M000166889

CREATOR

SUSTAINER

GOD

PROTECTOR

A BOOK
of
GOD'S LOVE

by

M. R. Bawa Muhaiyaddeen

THE FELLOWSHIP PRESS
Philadelphia, PA

Library of Congress Cataloging in Publication Data

Muhaiyaddeen, M. R. Bawa.
  A book of God's love.

  Discourses spoken in Tamil in Philadelphia
during February, 1980.
  1. Spiritual life. 2. God—Love. 3. Love. I. Title.
BL624.M82   291.4'4   81-4503
ISBN 0-914390-42-2   AACR2

Printed in the United States of America
by THE FELLOWSHIP PRESS
Bawa Muhaiyaddeen Fellowship
First Printing 1981
Second Printing 1987
Third Printing 1991
Fourth Printing 1994
Fifth Printing 1997
Sixth Printing 1999
Seventh Printing 2004

M. R. Bawa Muhaiyaddeen (*Ral.*)

Contents

Acknowledgements

This book is composed of several discourses given in Philadelphia during February of 1980 by M. R. Bawa Muhaiyaddeen, may God be pleased with him. These talks were given in Tamil, an ancient Dravidian language spoken in parts of India and Sri Lanka, and translated into English by Professor Ajwad Macan-Markar, Dr. M.Z. Markar, Dr. K. Ganesan, and Mrs. Crisi Beutler.

The entire production of this book from preparing the manuscript to the printing and binding was accomplished through volunteer work. Many members of the Bawa Muhaiyaddeen Fellowship gave their time, energy, skills, and financial support to make the wisdom of these words available for anyone who may be in need of their comfort.

Introduction

Dear Reader,

This is a book to lighten your heart, a map to help you find the treasure hidden within you. That treasure contains the most valuable and elusive things in life which everyone seeks but very few ever find—unconditional love, everlasting youth, and unchanging truth.

Those who wish to journey on this treasure hunt are invited to read this book. The author will beckon you as "my precious children" and within that lies your first clue, for this is a book of God's love spoken by a father to his children. To understand its meaning and unfold its secret, you must become a child. You must throw away the differences of an adult and regain the openness of a child. Only then will the words truly penetrate your heart.

So if you are ready, turn the page, open your heart, and begin your journey...

True Love

"Unless love is connected to God,
Unless it is connected to truth,
        to compassion, to justice, and to grace,
It is possible for it to break down."

*I*n the name of God, the Most Merciful, the Most Compassionate. *Amīn*. May all praise and all responsibility be given to that One God who is limitless grace and incomparable love. *Amīn*. May all the responsibilities in our life, the splendors, the highs and the lows, may they all be given to that One God, our Father who is goodness, love, and compassionate beneficence. *Āmīn*.

My very precious children, jeweled lights of my eyes, children born with me as the life within my life, the love within my heart, all my loving children who are the love within my love, who are mingled with my love, who dwell within my love, who are the wisdom within my wisdom, may God Himself protect us with His grace, bless us, and grant us an exalted life of excellence, good qualities, and good deeds. *Āmīn*.

My very precious children, I give you my love. My very precious children who are the life within my life, we have come to this world from our Father who is God. During the period when we existed as a soul composed of light, we knew our Father. When we were nothing other than light, that light perceived the Light; it prayed and bowed down in reverential obeisance. That light form still exists within us as a mysterious secret, a mysterious, secret light body, an atom, a ray, the soul. It is the treasure of wisdom which can be seen in the state of God's love. This soul, this light form is God's mystery, and its life is God's life. Its actions are God's actions, and its love is undiminishing, endless, and indivisible.

When we came to this world, we brought that form with us along with its actions, its behavior, its qualities, and its compassion. That is our mysterious secret. It is that love which makes us instinctively show compassion to others, makes us aware, and prompts us to soothe and comfort others. This quality of compassion is just one aspect of that light form. My precious children, we must realize that this compassionate love is a ray of God's infinite love, and we possess that quality of compassionate love, that resplendent light. The act of showing compassion toward others, that ray of light, the life which is the soul, that grace and wisdom are within us. God is within us and the secret story of the kingdom of God is within us. We must understand this.

My very precious children, what do we call love? The love we usually manifest is selfish. We might love a tree, but for selfish reasons. We raise a cow and love it. Why? For selfish reasons. We breed a horse, but what kind of love do we have for it? Selfish love, because it is our property. We keep a dog, and because it is *our* dog, we love it. We may look after a garden, grow a tree, keep a cat, or raise goldfish. No matter what we have or nurture, our love for it is selfish. If we have a friend, we have a motive for having that friend. Whether it is a friend, a house, whatever it may be, the love we manifest is selfish. No matter what we love, if we examine that love accurately we will find a selfish reason for it; we expect something in return. Even when we cling to a religion, a doctrine, racial prejudice, anything, if we examine our feelings carefully, we will always find that there is a reason behind those feelings—selfishness. All the different kinds of love we offer or observe have to be understood in this way.

Now, does this kind of love benefit us? No, it does not. The only love that is beneficial is selfless love. Whatever we raise or touch—cattle, goats, donkeys, horses, dogs, cats, rats, house, property, possessions, learnings, titles, fame, political status, or even wisdom—whatever it is we love, if our love is directed toward something and remains fixed on that thing, it is a love which can be lost, which can die. That love is not an intrinsically inner love like the fragrance in union with a flower.

Suppose we spread gravel on a roadway, level it, cover it with tar, and roll it perfectly flat and smooth. In the course of time, rain and snow will fall, trucks will drive over it, floods will overrun it, and eventually the road will crack and potholes will appear. The road stays perfectly level for a short while, but as the seasons change, potholes will appear. And if the wheel of a car falls into a pothole, the alignment may be ruined, the tire may be damaged, the axle might break, or something else could give way; there may even be an accident. Similarly, selfish love is subject to the changing seasons and tends to break down just as a road does. My very precious children, this is exactly how any kind of love that we foster within ourselves with selfish motives will end; it will break down sooner or later. Unless love is connected to God, unless it is connected to truth, to compassion, to justice, and to grace, it is possible for it to break down.

My very precious children, all the love manifested by the human race is exactly like this. If we pursue God, worship Him, ask Him for favors, for property, money, possessions, a baby, great titles, a kingdom, or even for heaven, if we love God with interested motives, with selfish love, that love will break down. It is a broken love. But God is limitless grace and incomparable love. His love has no selfish interests. His compassion, His actions, His conduct, His goodness, His love, and His compassionate qualities are shown equally to all living things. His love pervades everything, and He lives within all lives. Knowing each heart,

He does His duty; knowing the qualities of each life, He serves it; knowing the behavior of each life, He protects it.

My very precious children, this love which is God's love must take form within us. God's love must take shape within the human race. His love must be formed in our hearts. That state must begin to grow as a small embryo in our hearts. Before we give our love to anything, we must slice it open, examine it carefully, and change it into a love that is complete, unchanging, and offered properly without faults, shortcomings, or deceit. Our love must correspond point by point with His love. The love between one human being and another and the love between man and God must be a love in unity. Love and love must merge, grace and grace must merge, qualities and qualities must coincide, actions and actions must be identical. The grace here and the grace there must unite as one, this fragrance and that fragrance must merge. Just as the flower and its fragrance are one, two hearts must mingle as one. That alone can be called love. Only that kind of love has this delightful fragrance.

Every child must attain this state. Because man is the prince of God, when we place our faith in God, when we do our duty to others, to the human race, we must do it without attachment, without selfishness, in the proper way, expecting no reward. We must serve others with the firm belief that we are one family, that all human beings are our brothers and sisters, feeling the suffering of others as our own suffering, the sadness of others as our own sadness, the sorrow of others as our own sorrow, the illness of others as our own illness, the pain of others as our own pain, the hunger of others as our own hunger, the lives of others as our own life, and the happiness of others as our own happiness. My very precious children, love that pours forth like this is true love.

If we were to have the same kind of love for a man that we have for a tree, what good would that be? We might cultivate a teak tree with great love, but what happens when the price of teak goes up? We cut it down, don't we? We raise a beautiful horse, but if someone offers us a good price, we sell it. We raise a cow and consider it to be as precious as our own life, but if someone offers a high enough price, we sell it. We are capable of selling anything we love selfishly to get something in return.

We must reflect on the love we give each and every thing. Let us look at the condition of the human race today. If a man marries a beautiful woman or a woman marries a handsome man, if they have a beautiful child and do many things together lovingly, that certainly is looked upon as love by most people. Their two bodies joined and their two hearts merged and became one for awhile. But what is that love? It is physical love. It is selfish love and illusion. After a while, if the wife should fall ill, her husband will not take care of her. That same husband who promised so much love, saying they had one heart even though they had two bodies, now asks for a divorce. He does not want to look after her when she is ill, and his wife would probably also want a divorce in a similar situation. Is that love? No it is not. In true love, life must be shared. Illness, wealth, bodily suffering, happiness, joy, and sorrow must all be shared. Whenever there is love in which the husband and wife do not share everything equally, that love is born of selfishness. Only when everything is shared can it be called true love.

So, my very precious children, when you fall in love, analyze the state of that love. Cut it open, examine it carefully, and look for the love which is intermingled with love, the love born of wisdom, the love born of good qualities, the love born of good actions, the love born of good behavior, the love emanating from clarity. That is true love. Any other love is merely selfish, merely the love of physical beauty, of beautiful possessions or beautiful learning. When we give our selfish love to these things, that beauty will soon fade and our love will end. This love is like our love for cows and goats. When a man gives up one woman and takes another, or a woman gives up one man and takes another, that love was never, never true love.

My very precious children, just as the fragrance is inseparable from the flower, in true love two minds are joined together as one. This love must be brought into our conduct, our actions, our qualities, our tranquillity, and our wisdom, so that two can become one. Only when these qualities come together will true love flourish. We do not need selfish love. One life must mingle with another; one love must mingle with another. We have to trust and live in that state of love.

What is the point of loving God the same way we love a dog or a cat? When you sell the dog, you will have to sell God too. Can you transfer the love you have for a horse to God? If so, then when you sell the horse, you are selling God too. Is this not strange? Therefore, we have to learn the true meaning of love and put it into action. We have to learn what kind of love we must offer to God, what kind of love we must have in our lives, and what kind of love two people should have for each other. Their love must be like the flower and its inseparable fragrance. And what should our love for God be like? Our love of God must be a love of surrender, like one light surrendering to a stronger light. Love must surrender to love, wisdom must surrender to wisdom, grace must surrender to grace, our qualities must surrender to God's

qualities, our actions must surrender to His actions, our duties must surrender to His duties, our life must surrender to His life, and radiance must surrender to radiance. This means that man must become God, that God must surrender to God. Only the love which surrenders is true love. This is what true love really is.

When we speak of love, we speak as though we really had that love for all creations. We love the earth, we love the sky, we love the sun, the moon, fire, our bodies, cows, cats, trees, and flowers—we love everything. What is there we don't love? But this is all selfish love which we must transcend to learn what true love for God is in our lives. We must experience that unity and know what form of love should exist between a man and a woman. We must love each other as one race, one family. We must know that we are truly one community. This is the love we must discover. Life is to manifest that love in the same way that perfume emanates from a flower.

God's love transcends all these other so-called loves. His love is His conduct, His patience, His tolerance, His qualities, His actions,

14

His peacefulness, His compassion. True love is His *sabūr* or inner patience, His *shūkur* or absolute contentment, His *tawwakul* or surrender, and giving all praises to God, saying, "*Al-hamdu lillāh!*" God's love is His qualities of sympathy, generosity, mercy, the feeling that all lives are as precious as His own and that the hunger of all is His own hunger. His love permeates everything. We must have that kind of love. We must let that love take shape within us and surrender it to Him.

My very precious children, until that love exists within us, until that wisdom grows within us, until God's compassion is formed within us, until His actions grow within us, our love is a broken love. In this state, the love we offer God is like our love for dogs and cats. Our love of race, religion, doctrines, philosophies, possessions, money, wealth, and color is selfishly motivated. This love cannot be connected to God because it is broken love, a love which falls apart here and there.

Precious children, we have to understand what really constitutes love in our lives, and we have to understand the love we must have for God. That love knows neither comparison nor equal. We must have God's love for God and give His actions and His grace to Him. We must have God's compassion and attribute it to Him. We must have His conduct and attribute it to Him. We must show His qualities to Him, reach that state, and give Him that love. That is surrender.

Just as the fragrance and the flower are one, the soul and His mystery mingling together is love. The ray of our soul's light falling into His light is love. My very precious children, devotion to God is the surrender of our wisdom to His. Then we can learn. Only if our qualities surrender to His can we learn His qualities. Only if we surrender our life to Him, can we study His life, and only if we surrender our eyes and our intentions to Him, can we study His eyes and His intentions.

My very precious children, we must let His love and His actions work inside us this way. As long as we have prejudices, colors, religions, races, wealth, philosophies, books, and scriptures, and as long as we say, ''I am the best!

Mine! My possessions, my things, my relatives," as long as we hang on to these things, we cannot have that love which merges with God. Our love will be broken, like our love for dogs and cats. We may love a dog very much, yet we lead it around on a leash. We love a horse, yet we throw a saddle on it and ride it. We love a mule, yet we load it with bundles and ride it. What about our love for a cow? We take a big pail and milk it. And what love do we have for a tree? We carry a sack to pick its fruit. Selfish love always has a motive, and so we offer a different kind of love to each thing. This divided, selfish love vanishes once we no longer need that thing. If it doesn't have what we are looking for, our love disappears. This is a love that breaks and sees separations. Yet we keep saying there is love in our life, love of this and love of that. What kind of love are we talking about?

My very precious children, we must split open the love we have for each thing in our life and examine what is inside. We must open each tree, fruit, flower, our lives, our sexual pleasures, gold, our wealth, our houses, everything we look at with our eyes and our minds. If we dissect them all and look inside, we will eventually realize that there is only one kind of love, and that it is not something we see externally. When we truly perceive that wonder we will exclaim, "My God!" That love is 'my God', that wonder. That love which is at the core of everything we see is God. As we dissect everything what we ultimately see is 'my God'. This is love. Whatever it may be that we want to study or examine, if we cut it open, what we ultimately experience is the fragrance and the light which is 'my God'.

When we split open everything seen in life, finally we recognize that one thing which permeates all lives—God who appears as a ray, as the point at the center of everything. That point is love. And when we perceive that love present within all lives, we have to love that love. We exclaim, "Oh, my God, this is Your creation, how wonderful! This is Your food, how wonderful!" When we dissect anything, we see only His wonder inside. When we look at love, we see only His love; when we examine wisdom, we see only

His wisdom; when we study beauty, we see His beauty; when we analyze compassion, we see His compassion; when we observe any actions, we see His actions; when we see a miracle, we see Him as the miracle; when we perceive radiance, it is His radiance.

The love we should have is the love which looks at everything through Him. We must discover that love inside each and every thing we see. If we can find this and make it our own, then everyone will be a brother or sister born with us. This is the only kind of love in which God is present, the only love which is lasting. This is grace, this is wisdom and light. This love is the shining beauty of our face, the beauty of our heart, our wealth, our life. This is what makes our soul beautiful. This is what makes the house of our life beautiful. My very precious children, this beauty is love. May we each reflect on that love, may we open our hearts, look inside with understanding, and see that love. We must open our *qalbs*, our innermost hearts, and look within. We must dissect everything we understand, we must investigate everything we eat, we must examine our sleep, we must inspect the inside of everything we look at. Then we will see God's wonders and miracles. Then we will see this love which lives in all lives, which showers compassion on all lives, and we will say, "My God, how wonderful!"

My very precious children, each child must understand this, take this love into his heart, and use it in his life. We must all imbibe these qualities and these actions and put them to use in our lives. We must imbibe that duty and reveal it in our actions. We must draw that grace and that treasure within us. This love is true love, the love born of faith and trust, the love born of brotherly unity, the love that comes from being one family, the love that comes from prayer, the love that comes from merging with God, the love which has no limit. This love will never break or fail. It will never diminish or be destroyed no matter what storms or gales or destruction befall us. This unselfish, true love will never change or decrease.

My very precious children, we must dissect every thought we think, every wise thing we learn, every realization we receive, all the feelings we become aware of, all the clarity we experience, all the prayers we pray, all the scenes we look at, all the dreams we dream and our conduct by day and by night. We must dissect all this, look at it, and understand. Then from all this, we must extract love, truth, justice, integrity, honesty, and the laws of righteousness. We must discover these truths within that love and conduct our lives accordingly.

My very precious children, my children born with me, you must find the state of love which never perishes, which is God's love and His actions. My very precious children, you must realize this love in your faith, in your certitude, in your determination, in your wisdom, and in your clarity. Realize it as the clarity within clarity, as the wisdom within wisdom, as the divine wisdom within divine wisdom, as the grace within grace, as God within God. The love which mingles with God's love is true love, the actions are acts of love.

My very precious children, with what must we mingle, in what must we lose ourselves and to what must we connect ourselves? We must develop the love which mingles with God. My very precious children, may we develop that kind of love which will merge with Him. But how do we realize this love and faith, how do we act with God's actions and behavior, how do we perform our duty, how should we pray and worship?

If we want some light, though we may have oil and a wick, we still need a flame to light it. Unless we have a lighted match, the oil will remain oil and the wick will remain a wick. Only after we apply the match will the oil, the wick, and the flame become radiant light. My very precious children, our faith must be united with our wisdom. Only when they are one and God's light ignites them will we have light. My very precious children, we must have the oil called faith and the wick called wisdom, and we must bring God's light to ignite this wick. This is the light which will dispel the darkness and reveal His grace. May we reflect on this.

If each of you will open your heart, your actions, your wisdom, and your conduct and look within, you will see that every face is your face, every nerve is your nerve, each drop of blood is your blood, every sickness is your sickness, all hunger is your hunger, all poverty is your poverty, all sorrow is your sorrow, all lives are your life. You will experience all this in your nerves, in your body and in what you see. When that state develops inside you, that is God's love. That is God's true love because all suffering is His suffering, all sorrow is His sorrow, all hunger is His, all poverty is His, and all grief is His. Every torment is inside Him. This is how God does His duty. Therefore, if you develop that love, you will do your duty in the same way. If that love develops you will not hurt any other living thing, you will not cause pain, you will not reject any life, and you will not torture any other life, because if you hurt anyone it will hurt you.

My very precious children, look at a tree. It may have a thousand branches and a million leaves and flowers. If you cut any one of those flowers, leaves, or branches, the tree feels the pain, doesn't it? The leaves droop immediately, don't they? They wilt immediately because of the pain. See how the leaves wilt in the sun. If the leaves wither, the tree withers. If a branch falls, the tree feels the pain, isn't that so? A branch cannot fall without the tree being aware of it. The leaves don't wither or wilt without the tree being aware of it, because the tree holds on to them with a gluey substance. My very precious children, even though a tree has millions and millions of leaves and flowers, it feels the pain caused to each one by the rain, sun, and snow. In the same way, my precious children, when you realize who you are, when you develop those qualities yourself, all mankind will be like leaves glued to your body, all lives will be like your bark or covering, all suffering will be yours. The blood of others, the illness of others, the hunger of others will all be linked to you. Once you have God's love, God's qualities, and God's actions, everyone is connected to you, and therefore you will feel the suffering no matter whose it is. When you develop that fullness you will feel all the suffering there is.

If a good man can be like a tree, he will be a tree in the world of the soul, in this world and in the next. He will experience the suffering of the whole world, because it will all flow into him. All the illness, all the grief, all the hunger will be experienced by him. He will feel everything felt by every nerve, every tissue, and every muscle of everyone in the world. God sent every prophet in that state. He sent every prophet to assume the suffering of others, to relieve the suffering and illness of the world, to accept the karma of the world, to preach wisely, to make grace complete, and to dispel the darkness.

And so, my very precious children, when we reach that state, we will experience all the pain, the suffering, and the illness that exist. In that state everyone will be a brother or a sister, and we will feel every illness inside ourselves. My very precious children, you must realize what God's love is, what man's love is, what the meaning of love is, what the meaning of devotion is, what wisdom is, what the love we have for God is, and what is the love we are now experiencing. We must understand the differences between them. If we can identify and discover true love we will become representatives of God and live as the lights of God, as light intermingled with God. When that time comes, we will feel all the sorrows of the world within us.

My very precious children, each child, please think about this. We must realize our love, God's love, love of all people, brotherly love, love of justice, love of truth, love of honesty—this is what we must be aware of. May we reflect on this, my very precious children, jeweled lights of my eyes, may each child reflect on this, understand what wisdom is, and acquire that love. Conduct yourself as God conducts Himself. Show God's compassion to everyone. Have God's love for everyone. May we bring that love into practice. *Āmīn. Āmīn.*

My love to all my children, my love to all my precious children. Please forgive me if there is anything wrong in what I have said. I give you my love.

Forgiveness

"Until our very last breath, until we leave this world itself, God always holds out His hands to uplift us. He has His hands outstretched to embrace us, to give us His milk, and to teach us . . . Until that very last breath, we are never separated or apart from God."

*B*ismillāhir-Rahmānir-Rahīm. In the name of God, the Most Merciful, the Most Compassionate. May that God who is incomparable love and the unfathomable Ruler of grace, who gives us His never-ending wealth and grace, bless us all. Āmīn. May God, our Creator, watch over us, nourish us and protect us all our lives. Only God can do that. May He forgive all our faults with His grace. Amin. O God, please forgive the faults which we committed before we knew You. Āmīn. May this prayer be granted.

Jeweled lights of my eyes, precious children, you were born with me as the life within my life. Precious jeweled lights of my eyes, beloved of my heart, treasure of my eyes, children who are exalted and wise, brothers and sisters of my heart, my loving children who are so trusting, I give you my love and my greetings. Precious jeweled lights of my eyes born as my own brothers, you were indeed born with me. We have all come here together and it is important to know why we are here. First, we must understand right and wrong—that is the most important thing we must do. We should not dwell on the past, on old karma, on past sins, on the faults of a previous birth. We should never think that God will not forgive our faults and that we will be subject to rebirth. We must not think like that.

Children, we have to recognize that although God is not like us, He is our Father. He doesn't have our qualities, He doesn't think like us, He doesn't have our jealousy or pride, He is not self-ish, He has neither anger nor sin, and He does not look for praise, honors, or titles. God is patient, He is compassionate, He is tolerant, He is peaceful, He is just, He has perfect integrity. He is the One with three thousand beautiful qualities. He is the One who believes that other lives are His own and then does His duty. He is the One who recognizes the sorrows of others as His own and then does His duty. He is the One who understands right and wrong and then does His duty. He is the One who distinguishes truth from falsehood and then serves us and offers His explanation. He has good thoughts, He is the Father who created us, He is our God.

He does not punish us for our faults. He does not get angry, He does not forsake us, He does not send us away from Him, and He does not see differences among us. He is responsible for all lives, and He is patient. He is never angry with us, because we are His children. He forgives the faults we commit until we become wise and begin to understand our mistakes. He understands all the faults we committed while playing in ignorance, all the faults we committed both accidentally and purposefully, and all the lies we told. He understands them and always acts without anger or sin to protect His children. He makes wise men teach, because He wants His children to learn with awareness. He teaches us through our very thoughts, through the trees, the bushes, the vines, the animals, even through the sun and the moon. Through feeling and awareness He demonstrates what we need to know, turning us around and directing us to the path of truth, developing wisdom within us. He teaches wisdom through everything. He continually tries

31

to turn us around and re-direct us so that He can take us back and embrace us. His constant remembrance is to do this for us.

Precious jeweled lights of my eyes, He is the One who forgives the faults we commit in ignorance until we learn to recognize them as faults and give them up. God thinks, "They are only children acting in ignorance. Some day they will understand. I brought goodness into being, and I created right and wrong so that the difference between them might be understood. I created day and night so that my children would understand. I brought the body, soul, and light here so that my children would comprehend. I created wisdom and ignorance to develop their understanding.

"For this reason I created all the opposites, all the contrasts, to make them see both, to make them accept and act upon the truth and avoid evil. This is why I created both. Those children who know Me have My qualities and the capacity to extract the truth and use My wisdom. Yet even those who act in ignorance, without understanding, who accept what is wrong, are still My children. I am the only One who can judge either group, because I created them, and I have to make a place for both.

"There are so many creations, and I exist within them all as their inner awareness. In each heart I exist without shape, without form or color. I exist within as the power and the form of wisdom. Until they emerge from darkness, they will be ignorant and lack understanding. For this reason, I must forgive the faults they commit in that state.

"I have created so many forms: the sun, the moon, trees, bushes, weeds, birds, crawling animals, rats, flies, beetles, insects, the atoms themselves, energies, and forces. I created them all to make mankind understand, realize, and have faith."

Precious children, jeweled lights of my eyes, we must have faith in God, our Father. We must develop that faith with determination. We must establish certitude and make our faith very firm. That strength of faith will be a staff to support us and help us climb; it is the means to cross the desert without wavering. If we fall very far, we will need this staff to climb back up. If we have the faith and determination to understand that there is no God like our Father, then we can climb up, we can avoid evil, and we can act wisely and reach the place where wisdom exists.

Precious jeweled lights of my eyes, there is room for realization. There is something to learn from every created thing. There are many, many explanations to understand. Precious jeweled lights of my eyes, everything we see teaches us wisely. Everything we see is there for us to understand and to give us peace in that place of understanding. All the forces and miracles and the power which can rule them have been given to us by God. The wisdom and tranquillity with which we can rule the earth and the sky have been given to us. The most exalted beauty, the most exalted qualities, and the most exalted wisdom, tranquillity, peace, justice, and integrity have been given to us. We can understand through our birth and our death. We have to realize that the explanation of wisdom lies within us. We have to understand this.

Our Father is never angry with us. He never

says, "I will send him to hell. I will test him and then send him to hell." He forgives us just as we forgive our own child if he misbehaves. We forgive him; we don't hate or destroy him, or cast him away. If we would not do such things in our state of ignorance, if we treat our children with compassion, how do you think God who has true wisdom would behave? We are angry and hasty, but we take care of our own children, and protect them even if they are wrong. We have so many bad qualities, we are so selfish, we are so engaged in the business of the self, we have so many prejudices concerning religion, race, and color, yet we are still able to protect and care for our own children lovingly. How much greater must God's love be! God, who is the unfathomable Ruler of grace, the One who is incomparable love, the One who gives us the wealth of His grace without end, how much greater must His love be! What is the nature of His love? Does He get angry? Does He hate us? Does He test us? He does nothing of the kind. The evil and the mistakes are all inside ourselves. When we act in ignorance, we plunge ourselves into danger.

When we behave unwisely, our own faults subject us to accidents and danger. We have to live with the consequences of our own faults, our own actions, and our own qualities.

Our Father doesn't test us or get angry with us. He gave us eyes so that we can walk looking ahead. He gave us ears to hear with and a nose to smell both good and bad scents. He gave us a tongue to distinguish good tastes from bad and a mouth to utter good words. We must realize the difference between good and evil, and then use the tongue He gave us to speak about the good. He gave us limbs, hands, legs, hearts, and bodies. We have to understand this, precious jeweled lights of my eyes. We have to use our eyes to recognize good and evil. If we do not understand, we may fall into a hole. That will not be God's fault, will it? Certainly not. We are the ones who have fallen into the hole. We are the careless ones. We cannot blame God. We have to consider the sounds we hear, both good and bad. We have to shun the bad, accept the good, and guide our actions accordingly. If we act on the basis of evil sounds, we are looking for an accident.

There are good smells and bad smells. It is correct to pursue the good fragrances. If we associate with the bad smells, we will have to experience the evil from which they come. There are good words and bad words on the tongue. If we use the good words, we will know the taste of peace; if we use the evil words, sin and evil will follow. Is this God's fault? It is our own fault. We must recognize good and bad tastes and spit out what is bad. We must absorb the good tastes, but if we eat the bad food, it will hurt us. Whose fault is that? Is that God's fault? Certainly not!

We must reflect. Precious jeweled lights of my eyes, our Father does not get angry with us. He does not test us. He is total power, the mysterious One. Would that power test us? Could we bear His test? Are we that strong? We are very small. We are only a particle of a particle of a particle, and He is greater than all the universes. He is the great power, creating, destroying, and watching over all lives. If that power which can make the world appear or disappear in the blink of an eye were angry with us, what could we do? But that power is our Father. What indication is there that He would hurt us? What indication is there that He would test us? Could we bear anything He might do? Could we endure it, could we withstand His test? We have to consider this wisely.

Precious jeweled lights of my eyes, He is love, He is compassion, He is patience, He is tolerance and peace and above all His creations. He is our Father. We have to understand that He is God and that He has no anger. He does not try to punish people or send them to hell. He is clear wisdom who always trusts and believes that we will return to Him. Until a child grows to be good, until he sets out on the true path, God tries to comfort him, teach him true wisdom, and find a teacher for him. It is for this reason that God sent the prophets, the lights of God, the *qutbs*, the wise men, and the *rasūls*. They were sent from His kingdom to His children to dispel the ignorance, to dispel the lack of wisdom and the darkness so that God's children might acquire His qualities and turn to the path of truth. God always says, "May the children search for their Father. May they come to Him." Let us think about this.

This is God's endless work. Through the wise men, the *qutbs*, the lights of God, the saints, the holy men, and the prophets, He brings His children to realization. With the sun and the moon and in so many different ways, He develops their wisdom, dispelling their darkness to make them return to Him. Precious children, God is trying to bring us to this realization step by step. That is our Father's nature. We have to understand that He will forgive us until the end. As our wisdom grows, as we realize our faults, we can ask for forgiveness, and He will grant it. As we recognize our faults, He will forgive us and accept each of us as His own child. We must reflect on this wisely and understand it.

We must be good and avoid evil. We really must strive. If we do not, we will fall into evil ways, and justice will be carried out in that place of final judgment. But until then, God will teach us as much as He can through every creation—through the reptiles, the sun and the moon, currents and magnetism, gold and silver, the earth, wealth, trees and flowers, fragrance, medicine, everything. It is God who teaches us through everything. It is God who makes us correct ourselves and turns us back to the true path. He is always patient. He is never angry with us, He never hates us, He never tries to cast us away, and He never tests us. God only shows us His grace. Let us consider this wisely.

Precious jeweled lights of my eyes, God also created satan. Couldn't God destroy him? Why did He give satan so much power in hell? Can't He vanquish satan? Can God overcome him? He can indeed overcome anything, so why did God create a satan? Good and evil are the responsibility of Allah, exalted be His name. Good and evil, light and darkness were created by God so that we might be brought to realization. Until then, until that day, God has to make room for satan. Why? Because satan was created too. God created satan and He will not destroy him. He is not angry with him. Does God destroy us, does He hate us, does He test us? We have to realize that God created satan too, but He also created a Judgment Day at the end of it all, and on that day He will grant heaven or hell according to what each one has searched for. At that time the

41

house of hell will be given to satan, and that is where he will live.

Precious jeweled lights of my eyes, there are many lessons to learn. There are so many things to filter and learn from the earth, from water, air, fire, and ether. There are so many things to be understood from reptiles, bushes, and trees. There are so many things we have to understand. God has created each thing. He protects it, and He will continue to forgive it until that final judgment comes. Precious jeweled lights of my eyes, we have to realize, understand profoundly, and be clear about the truth. We must realize that once we know our Father, everything we did earlier will be forgotten. Those were unwitting actions performed in a state of ignorance; they were faults we committed when very young. The faults we commit before wisdom emerges are all the faults of our youth. With wisdom comes maturity. Before that we are all small, very immature children even though our bodies may be large. If we realize this wisdom before we die, we can know our Father. But if we do not become wise and turn to the path of wisdom before we die, then we will become darkness.

Until our very last breath, until we leave this
world, God always holds out His hands to uplift
us. He has His hands outstretched to embrace
us, to give us His milk, and to teach us awareness. He is inside our hearts, cleansing us. Until
the very last breath He embraces each child,
trying to bring that child to Him. He strives for
this until our very last breath. But if we lose the
opportunity to develop our wisdom, if we remain
with satan in a state of ignorance until our last
breath, then we will be found guilty and subject
to punishment. We will be separated from God.
But until that very last breath, we are never separated or apart from God.

God does not get angry with us, He does not
hate us, He does not test us. Precious jeweled
lights of my eyes, we have to realize that our
Father will forgive all the faults we committed
when we were ignorant, and He will not be
angry. We must believe this with certitude. We
have to understand very profoundly, precious
jeweled lights of my eyes, that is why God sent
the wise men and the prophets. After He had

sent all the prophets, God sent the *qutbs* and messengers. At any time there is always at least one *qutb*, one wise man, in the world. Through him we must learn to be wise, we must understand the truth, and we must acquire the recognition of what is good so that we can protect ourselves from danger. Therefore, precious jeweled lights of my eyes, search for wisdom. Search for that wisdom which is your birthright. Search for the birthright your Father gave you. Search for that property He gave you. We must intend to return to that place where we lived before. We must try to re-unite with our Father and have His qualities and His actions. We must try to behave as He behaves and make His duty our own. We must act with our Father's patience, we must try to nourish His unity, receive His beauty, and act with His qualities.

Precious jeweled lights of my eyes, children who are my very life, you must travel the path of integrity with absolute certitude and really try to search for wisdom. This is most important. Just because we committed mistakes earlier, we should not go on thinking we have done so many horrible things and have so many faults. We have not committed any faults in the eyes of God. We are small children to Him, and He will always forgive us. He will not hate or discard us. We have to think of this until our very last breath. We have to search for wisdom and act as truth dictates. Then, when we become wise, we will not commit our earlier mistakes, and we will not walk the paths we traveled earlier.

We do have many faults when we have no wisdom. We do make mistakes, and we have to realize this. Precious children, understand this. Try to live in a good way, associate with good people and adopt their qualities. Find a wise man and try to become wise. Because God is love, because He is just, because He is compassionate and patient, we must try to do this. Then we will have peacefulness, tranquillity, and justice. We will have attained the birthright of our eternal life.

Precious children, we must realize that we have to know and understand ourselves. We must stop playing. We must try to walk the true path and realize that God will forgive our faults, and He will be tolerant of all our mistakes. Then we will become His children, His babies, and He will give us His kingdom. He will give us His house and His grace. God will give us all His treasures. We have to realize this, precious jeweled lights of my eyes. The world is a lesson to help us realize what we have to know. Everything God created is a lesson, an explanation we have to understand.

We must understand everything. Precious jeweled lights of my eyes, we must understand and then we must act on that understanding. It is very easy to talk about this, but we must act accordingly. We must strive as wisely as we can to put this state into action. We must open our hearts and look within. We must open our hearts and understand what that wisdom is, what the tranquillity of that wisdom means, and we must establish this in our lives. This is the secret of life, the birthright of our lives, the completeness, the happiness, and the exaltedness of our lives. This is the state we must attain. We must understand our God, our Father, our Lord, our Allah, exalted be His name, our *Rabb*, our Creator, and we must find Him. We must find the wisdom, the tranquillity, and the qualities to do that. We must acquire His beauty.

Precious children, this is what we must earnestly strive to do. Each one must think, each heart must realize. We must understand, and we must ask our Father to forgive us. When our wisdom emerges, we will be able to speak happily with our Father and become one with Him. As soon as we embrace Him, He will forgive our faults. He will not hate us, He will accept us and say, ''My child, now you are wise. My child, now you are a loving child. You have taken My qualities, you have compassion for all lives, and you perform My duty. Now you are My child, now you are My son. Now your sound is My sound, now your speech is My speech, now your actions are My actions, now your conduct is My conduct, now your qualities are My qualities and your wisdom is My wisdom. Now your actions, your behavior, and everything about you has found My duty. My son, now My sound and resonance have arisen within you.'' Then He will embrace you, saying, ''Now you are My son.''

We must try to find that beauty and those qualities, precious children, jeweled lights of my eyes. We must transform our lives, merge with our Father, and strive to find that wisdom and tranquillity. We need faith, determination, and certitude; we need that *imān* which is absolute faith. We must labor to know clearly that God is our Father. We must have the certitude that there is no other God, we must know that He is the Only One, we must know absolutely that we are one family and that God is our only Father. We must understand, show compassion for all lives, and have that certitude. That is the most exalted path of grace. May each one of us remember, may we all understand this and act upon it. May we actually do this. *Āmīn. Āmīn.*

As-salāmu 'alaikum wa rahmatullāhi wa barakātuhu kulluhu—May the peace of God and His beneficence be upon all of you. Love to all the children, love to everyone, love to all the jeweled lights of my eyes. If there is any fault in what I said, please forgive me. I am still a student with no wisdom. Please forgive me if there is any fault in what I have said.

Cultivating
the
Heart

"Prayers that come from the heart and actions that come from the heart go directly to Him. Nothing else will be of any use to you at all, my precious children."

Āmīn. Āmīn. May we surrender all responsibility to God, the limitless Ruler of grace and incomparable love. *Āmīn.* May our life, its exaltedness, the good times and the bad be His responsibility. *Āmīn.* May He be responsible for our birth, our life, and our death, and for the good and evil we do. May He alone be responsible for the exaltedness of our life, for the grace that will take away our sorrow, and for the duty that will make us grow and bring us to the other shore. *Āmīn.*

My very precious children, jeweled lights of my eyes, fellow beings who are the life within my life, the source of my eyes' light, my loving children who melt my heart, I give you my loving greetings. May God comfort us and give us His grace. *Āmīn.* Let God alone be responsible for everything in our life and for its splendor. May He nurture us on the true path. May He feed us His good qualities and give us His grace, His treasure, His limitless wealth. May He feed us the milk of His love and pour the honey of His grace into us. May He show us the light of wisdom and teach us to understand the secrets of the three worlds. May He show us the straight true path. May He grant us His grace and embrace us with the wealth of His grace. *Āmīn*.

My loving children, my jeweled lights, consider the world, this earth. We have lands and oceans, jungles and huge mountains. There are places where you can farm, places where you cannot, and places where the soil is rich but of no use because it has not been cultivated. Some earth is salty, some is red, and some is black or various other colors. Brass, copper, iron, sulphur, oil, and precious gems are all found in the earth, but they cannot be found everywhere. There are rocks everywhere, but not precious gems. Water is everywhere, but in some places it is not at the surface. You might find water where none is evident if you dig very deep, but you have to make a great effort to reach it. There is no place without earth, without water, without air, without fire, or without illusion. The elements exist in the earth, in the skies, in the seven lower worlds, and in the seven heavens above. But precious gems, my children, do not exist everywhere.

Earth is found everywhere, but can we grow crops just anywhere? Water is everywhere, but can we drink just any water? Air is everywhere, but can we inhale just any air? Fire is everywhere, but can we use fire just anywhere? Illusions are found in abundance everywhere, but do we accept them all? There is land everywhere, but can we build a house just anywhere? No, we cannot.

My very precious children, these things are all available, but we must know which crop will grow in which soil and what kind of fertilizer is needed. We must know where we can find gems, where the oil is, where the lead is, the copper, the gold, iron ore, silver, mercury, and sulphur. We must examine the earth to discover which stones contain gems, we must examine the world to discover which water will quench our thirst, and we must analyze the air we breathe to know which gases are beneficial or essential.

This is the way we have to search for God too. We have to scrutinize the gurus and sheikhs we meet. We have to discover where the wisdom we need exists, what sort of wisdom can be found where, and what wisdom truly is. Just as it is necessary to find the correct place for whatever we need to do, we must also find the place where we can discover that which is of true value, the place from which we can reach God and acquire His qualities, His treasure, and His wisdom. My very precious children, we must examine all this.

There are millions of gods which take the name of God, millions of religions which take the name of God, and millions of languages and histories which claim to speak in God's name. So many people put on different robes, clothing, and emblems in God's name. Many such things have been brought into existence in God's name, but on this farm, this world where everything is available, we must cultivate our crops. We must cultivate the land and examine the soil to know which crops will grow. We must find the land that we can live on and build our house, and we must find water which is drinkable. We must think about all these things.

My children, if you need a well, you might have to dig two to find one with good water. And you might have to dig twenty, forty, one hundred, or even one thousand feet just to find two springs. If those springs are good, the water will well up continually. If they are not, either your well will dry up very soon or the water level will drop in one season and rise in another. But if you dig your well in the correct place which is not affected by the changing seasons, water will always be available. You have to dig the well in the right place.

There is endless water in the ocean, but can we drink it? No we cannot. The water in the ocean never diminishes but it is not drinkable. Similarly, there is so much water in a lake, but if you just boldly walk in, you may drown. And after all your digging, can the amount of water in a well compare with the amount in a pond? No, but the pond water contains germs, dirt, and fungi. You cannot drink it directly; it has to be cleaned first, because so many things are mixed in it. Once you examine it, you will discover all the dirt and the stench in that pond. Then how can we drink its water? We have to filter it first.

My very precious children, the world is within us. Just as there are different kinds of water, there are different kinds of knowledge. You will find religions, scriptures, and philosophies as deep as the ocean. There are languages as vast as the ocean. There are so many different alphabets—Hebrew, Arabic, English, or Telugu, for example—and so many countless languages, like Greek, Kerandhum, Pali, Urdu, Hindi, Waduhu, Bengali, and so on. There are many, many languages, but can we benefit from them? Can we see God through these letters? Can we see God through the words we learn? Can we know God through any of our races even though they are as vast as the ocean? Although the earth is everywhere, can we plant crops anywhere? No we cannot. Can we inhale any air indiscriminately? If we breathe the air coming from a toilet, we will fall ill. It is air, but we cannot breathe it. Fire is everywhere, but if we try to confine every fire into one place, it will burn us up. Can we bake break anywhere? Can we dig a well or find a spring just anywhere? No we cannot.

My very precious children, we see countless things every day which are of no benefit to us. Do we acquire wisdom through the alphabet? If we study Hebrew do we acquire wisdom? Do we acquire wisdom through Arabic or English? Do we merge with God? No, we cannot achieve that state through languages. They are like the waters of the ocean, salty and incapable of quenching thirst. None of them can benefit us; none of this water can be used to cultivate a good crop.

Can we reach God with race, religion, color, prejudice, and discrimination? Can we grow a true crop of wisdom through such channels? No we cannot. Only after examining the soil can we determine where to grow which crop. Only after examining the water can we determine whether it is pure. We have to examine each place to determine its shortcomings and then find a healthy, clean environment in which to live and build our house.

This is why we have to consider everything and examine each condition. It is essential and urgent to analyze each little detail. We have everything. We have all these languages, yet languages, colors, and words—this kind of cultivation is of no use to us. Books and stories, like the waters of the ocean, are of no use to us. We cannot grow that crop of wisdom with these.

Cells, viruses, energy, mercury, sulphur, gold, and silver are all found in many different places, but who knows where? Only God knows, because He is the only One who does not need any of these. He does not need gold, He does not need gems or mercury, He does not need anything, and that is why He knows everything that exists everywhere. The One who needs nothing knows everything; the One who has discarded everything perceives everything. He knows every bit of the earth and the seas. He knows every language, all the scriptures, religions, colors, races, metals, and gold. He knows all about them, but He does not want them. He has pushed all these away and does not even think about them. He does not try to acquire these things. He takes no interest in our languages, our colors, our racial prejudice, our gold, titles, honors, or knowledge. He is not interested in our praise or blame, in our earnings, our wealth, or our histories. He has discarded all this. And because He has discarded everything, He is complete everywhere.

My precious children, jeweled lights of my eyes, from the time you are one month old until you are a year and a half or two years old you speak many, many different languages. You speak the languages of all God's creations, yet your parents do not understand or pay attention. Until they teach you to understand their own language, they do not understand yours; it is completely incomprehensible to them.

An infant speaks a thousand languages when he says, "Aaah, mmmnn." He knows every language, but although his parents spoke that way too at one time, they have forgotten. As the child grows, it learns the temporary language of the parents and forgets that original one. The parents teach their child, "We are Arabic. We are Hebrew. We are Telugu. We are English." They teach these temporary languages and the original one leaves. The child acquires the separation of 'you' and 'I', and is taught the relationships of *my* father, *my* uncle, *my* grand-father.

Well, my children, even though we study many languages, they are of no use to us at all. We knew them once before as children and forgot them. Each language is spoken in a specific place. Birds have their languages, all the animals have their languages. Bees have their own language, as do rats, deer, monkeys, men, and donkeys. The child knows and speaks them all. Who taught him this? The child speaks that non-specific language which is found throughout the world. All God's creations speak this language. The whole world is within the child: the different gases, all those languages, gold, gems and the light of those gems. Grace, beauty, light, and God are inside him too. Everything exists in totality within the child. Even heaven and hell are within him. He must start to examine all these things.

If a child could retain that original speech, he would speak a universal language which everyone understands. And because he could speak everyone's language, he would have no sense of differences. He would think of all lives as his own. Everyone would be his brother or sister. He would trust everyone and love everyone. He would show compassion to every living creature, because he would speak their language and understand. Knowing that original language would enable him to do that. But because he has forgotten this and has learned a temporary language, he thinks, "I am great. This is my religion, that is your religion."

My very precious children, my jeweled lights, we have a world inside us, we have five different gases in us, we have desire which is illusion inside us, gold, mercury, and every conceivable thing. We have every language inside us. So what must we do? We must start by examining this earth within our hearts to discover which crops can be grown there, what kind of cultivation are we capable of, what can we cultivate that will be of use to us, which languages are we going to speak, which language can we use to invite God to us. We have to start digging into these things to understand them. We have to examine and analyze them to discover where the wisdom, the light, and the completeness originate. Once we sort and examine these things, we will discard everything that is not useful, just as God, knowing everything, discarded everything. Once He created everything, God discarded everything. He is humble and all-pervasive, doing His duty to everyone, everywhere. God does not take any of His creations for Himself. He has given up everything, yet He does His duty to everything. He wants no praise, He is neither selfish nor proud, He has no 'I', no 'you', He has none of this. He learned all there is to learn and then discarded it all.

God knows every language and He has discarded them all. He knows every alphabet and He has let them all go. He has let everything go except for one point which is His. That one point is wisdom, and that one point connects us to God. He wants none of our literature or languages, He wants only that atom contained within our hearts. There is a connection between this atom and the mysterious power inside it. God has given up everything else, so what can He do with the languages you offer Him? He has given up literature, so why offer Him writings? He has given up gold, so why try to offer Him gold? He has given up precious gems, so why offer Him gems? What would He do with them? He has given up races, so what can He do with the race you offer Him? He has given up religions, so what can He do with the religion you offer Him? He has given up colors, so what can He do with the color you offer Him? He has given up praise, so what is the point in flattering Him? He has given up selfishness, so what can He do with the selfishness we give Him?

Can we reach that One who has given up countless objects by offering Him what He has discarded? We can never return to Him or merge with Him that way. God has none of that, yet He is complete within each thing He has given up. There is no place where God is not, there is nothing He does not see, nothing He has not created, no justice He has not determined, no life He has not fed. He feeds the grass, the weeds, the shrubs, the evil people, and those who are in hell. He feeds the food of hell to those who are in hell. He feeds the earth with earth.

He feeds those who possess the truth with truth, those who have wisdom with wisdom, and those who have His grace with grace. To those who have surrendered to Him, He feeds Himself. He feeds the earth with earth, He feeds water with water, He feeds animals with animals, He feeds insects with insects, He feeds ants with ants, He feeds termites with termites, He feeds fish with fish, and He feeds His food to those who have surrendered to Him.

Each species or category in His creation is fed with the specific food God has reserved for it. That food becomes its own particular food. If we try to hang on to hell, He feeds us the things of hell. If we are arrogant He feeds us arrogance, if we are patient He feeds us patience, if we are wise He feeds us wisdom, if we are truthful He feeds us truth. Truth is the food of the truthful. Our wisdom is God's food, and God's grace is our food.

We must investigate and analyze everything that happens, my precious children. Religion, philosophy, literature, color, race, and scriptures are of no use to us because God has none of that.

We are all His children. He is the Father of all His creation. And because He is our Father, He feeds and nourishes us so that we may grow. He is the Father of the grass, the bushes, the sun, the moon, of everyone, of every life. There is only one Father for each and every creation, for each of His countless creations. He provides for them all without attachment. He gives them everything, but nothing He provides remains within Him. He does His duty to everything, but receives nothing from them in return.

My precious children, there is one point for which we must dig with our wisdom, our faith, our prayers, our worship, and our *'ibādat*, our devotion. If we want to return to God and merge with Him, then we must examine ourselves and look for that point. We must discard everything from ourselves just as our Father did. The day we do this, we will merge with Him. When we no longer have these colors, races, religions, languages, and literatures inside us, we can meet Him. But if instead, we bundle together the things He has discarded and offer them to Him, He will not accept them. He will throw them away. He threw these things away before and He will throw them away again. If we offer Him our languages, He will throw them away. If we offer Him our colors, He will throw them away. If we offer Him our races, He will throw them away. If we offer Him our gold or our illusion, He will throw them all away. None of these are of use to us.

If we try to profit from the languages we have learned, from the knowledge we have acquired, from our religion or race, nothing will come of it, because God has no use for anything selfish. He does not fight, He has no prejudice, no arrogance, no anger. He does not discriminate. He has no ego. He has none of this. And now that we have separated ourselves from the One who has none of these attributes, how can we return to Him? By imbibing His qualities of patience, tolerance, and tranquillity, and putting them into action. We can come close to God through His qualities. When our wisdom develops and our determination accepts His treasures, we will know God. Until we have the wisdom to acquire that knowledge, our religions, races, and colors will only end in a battle which will destroy our nation, the world, our life, and our birth. That battle will destroy our compassion, our patience, our unity, and our family. This war will destroy our connection to that One God.

It is very difficult to reach God if we have all these wars going on inside. With our devotion in that state, with our faith in that state, with our prayer, meditation, and worship in that state, we can never return to God because He has no battlefield, no armies, no discrimination, no prejudice. He does not notice whether someone is black or white. He gave us the original languages we spoke earlier. Everyone speaks those languages; earth, fire, water, air, and ether all speak those languages. There is a musical note in the air, ''Aahaahaahaah.'' You hear those sounds in the air don't you? ''Oohoohoohooh.'' You can hear that sound in water, can't you, and ''Shhhhhhhhhh,'' the sound in fire. You can hear these sounds in the earth when it quakes, erodes, and resounds, and in the sky when lightning appears and it thunders. All those colors are found in the ether, in maya. All these things are visible, they all exist, do they not? But we cannot go to God with the things we see around us, with the things which exist everywhere.

We have water within us, and fire, and earth, and air. We have ether, colors, and illusions within us. We all have all of this. None of it has left any of us. So what basis do we have for discrimination and prejudice? Satan is in our bile. We all have black dots in our pupils, some have black hair, and some wear black clothes. Everything exists within us. If we want to fight, we have to fight parts of our self first. We have to fight our liver, we have to fight our nostrils. Every color is inside us, blue, black, green, and we have to fight them first. Once we finish those wars, that will most certainly be the end. But if we keep all that inside us, what is the point in fighting on the outside and discriminating against others on the basis of language? Some people feel nauseated when they hear Arabic. Others feel sick when they hear Hebrew, others when they hear English or Tamil or Telugu. Why should these languages make people feel sick?

When you retch that way only your own gut comes out. The nauseated person is the one who suffers. As long as we retain whatever makes us feel that nausea, we will experience pain.

Why should we carry our houses on our heads? Enter your house when you need to and come back out again. Do your work, sleep, or sit there, but why should you carry it around? God does not have a house, does He? True knowledge is understanding all this. It will come when you begin to analyze things, when a good crop grows inside you, when the strength of wisdom grows in you, and when you begin to surrender. What does surrender mean? Does it mean going away somewhere to die? No, it is the state in which our *qalb*, our innermost heart, joins with God's in perfect faith, saying, "O my God, none of these actions are mine, everything I do belongs to You. There is no place where You are not. All my suffering begins with not seeing You. All my suffering begins with holding on to things inside myself that You do not keep inside You. O God, take everything away from me that You have removed from Yourself. I need nothing other than

Your path. Everything I have which You do not causes me such sorrow, suffering, pain, woe, and misery. It is hell. O God, please remove from me those things that are not in You, whatever they may be. O my Father, please accept me, and let everything inside me fall away." That is surrender.

It is our duty to surrender all responsibility to God. Nothing else will do us any good. When will you begin to acquire wisdom? When will you see God? When will you merge with your Father? You will never return to Him through literature, languages, or other such things. You will never find God with the things you keep inside. Discard everything which is not within our Father, and try to bring Him only those things He has in Himself. All the languages you studied, whatever language you pray in, all this is like the salt water of the ocean which can never quench your thirst. You perceive it as water, yet you cannot even bathe in it. The only thing it is good for is to relieve the itching of your body. Salt water is very useful for those who have itching bodies. It is good for the itch of your mind. It is good for illu-

70

sion or maya which keeps itching to go to the seashore, but it cannot help us come to our Father. To do that we must acquire His qualities and wisdom. Anything else is like the ocean water which will never quench our thirst. All the religions, racial, doctrinal, and linguistic wars, all the fighting because of our birth or our death will never be of any use to us in a million years, because none of these things are found with our Father.

We must analyze ourselves and find God within us. We must have His wisdom. Just as we extract electricity from water, we must take the light from that light of God, take the grace from His grace, extract our Father from our Father. This is what we have to take from Him. This is the most important thing we have to do. That point must merge with that point. Everything else can be discarded. We must think about this.

Precious jeweled lights of my eye, we must come to that place where there is firm determination, wisdom, and prayer, where the Father and His children are together as one. We should think about this. Until that state emerges within us, our knowledge is like a mirage, and all the languages and everything else we have learned in our life is like oil poured on fire. Our knowledge is like oil poured on fire, useless because it will burn. Our actions are like oil poured into hell, like throwing all the decent things we sought in our lives into hell. This is what it is like in hell. Precious jeweled lights, all our flattery, honors, positions, ego, religions, races, writings, and battles are oil poured into hell. Discriminating between this one and that one, between us and them, discriminating on the basis of color—all this is fuel for hell. When you pray with these things, you pray with the oil of hell.

My very precious children, think about this. We have to look within ourselves to see our Father here, within our hearts. We must have God's qualities here in the place where He lives, because the qualities of our Father are here. God's actions must be performed here because He acts here in our hearts. God's light must enter our hearts, and we must bring that light-explanation into action in our hearts. His grace, His treasure, and His house must be built in our

hearts. Only then will He live there. This work must be performed here in the heart. We must realize this point for He will let everything else go. This is His point, this is His light which is connected to us. This point is a light, a treasure which exists in everything.

Prayers that come from the heart and actions that come from the heart go directly to Him. Nothing else will be of any use to you at all, my very precious children. Knowledge that does not come from your heart, knowledge or the ability to speak is of no use to you—no matter what you may acquire in the world. Even if with great difficulty you should learn to meditate, or even if you find a spring, your well will run dry when the weather turns warm. When there is a lot of rain and snow the water level will rise, but in hot, sunny weather, your well will go dry. There will be no spring and no water. That kind of knowledge is easy, just saying something is easy, that kind of action is easy, that kind of meditation is easy, like finding springs on the surface of the earth. But you must understand that in the next season the water level will drop and all of these things will be useless. Your knowledge will be useless, your languages, your meditation and your wisdom will be useless. Everything will leave you.

You must find that deep, true spring which is eternal. You must discover the spring which will supply you with water for countless seasons, eternally. And you must distinguish this spring from the springs which rise and fall seasonally. To come to that eternal spring we must go deep, right to that original point, to God. When we reach that point, three springs will appear from which the water will flow eternally. You can never lose that treasure because what comes from those springs is God's point. God has discarded everything else. Only His grace will flow from there, eternally.

Precious children, jeweled lights of my eyes, we must think about this. None of the things God has discarded are of any use to us. What we hold onto is the oil which is the fuel for the fire of hell. Our prayers, our worship, our learning, titles, and honors are all merely the oil used to keep the fires burning in hell. Therefore, try very hard to dig deep and find the place which connects you to your Father.

When will we reach that point? When will we have tranquillity? When will we have peace? When will we discard all the things that are not our Father? Only when we have abandoned all these fights over language and all these religious battles, only then will we receive that treasure from God. My very precious children, my jeweled lights, this treasure is called wisdom. It is called grace. We must find that place and release those springs which will flow with the grace of our Father, the grace of His light and His wisdom.

Precious children, nothing else will be of any use to us. What point is there in working hard for anything else? That is inviting the very disease which will destroy us. We must discard these things, my children, and go on the path to God. We must try very hard to find that one true place. That will be good, my children.

My love to you. *Āmīn. Āmīn.* I give my love to all my children. My love and my greetings. If there is any fault in what I have said, please forgive me. My love.

Eternal Youth

"When we live as little children and behave as little children, what do we find? We find peace and tranquillity. We find the unity and love which embraces everyone. We may totter and fall while embracing each other, but we will do so in unity and love."

Amīn. O God, You are peace. *Amīn.* May You grant us peace with Your grace. *Amīn.* O God, You are limitless grace and incomparable love, You give us the never-ending wealth of grace, You are our Father. How can we ever praise You? You who have no equal, You who cannot be compared with any visible example, how can we ever praise You? You are that boundless love and grace. O God, You accept love as love without accepting praise as praise. How can we return Your love and Your compassion, O God? What can we do in return for Your love, Your duty, and Your actions undertaken without the slightest attachment or partiality?

Allah, exalted be Your name. O God, You fill each heart so full, and no matter how much we take, You are not diminished by even one drop. O God, You are the ocean of love, the ocean of wealth and grace, the ocean of good actions, qualities, and duties, aspect after aspect, each infinite and limitless. Even if each creation fills the vessel of its heart with You, Your qualities, actions, goodness, compassion, and virtue remain full forever. They are not diminished by even a single drop.

Almighty One, ever complete in His duty, *Ill-Allāhu*, You are God, the One who is alone, who has no hunger, who was never born, who has no illness, no desire, no maya, no mind, no confusion, the One who is life within all life, doing His duty for every life in His creation. O my *Rabb*, my Lord, mighty and pure, You are my Creator, the One who is complete perfection. My Father, with what tongue can we praise You? Can this tongue ever be sufficient? My God, may You bless us with the full and perfect way to worship You. *Āmīn*.

My very precious children, jeweled lights of my eyes, born with me as the body within my body, children born as the life within my life, my precious children who are the light of my eyes, my very precious children who comfort me as the heart within my heart, my loving children who are the one true life among the six kinds of lives in God's creation, my precious children, may God protect and sustain us. *Āmīn*. May God protect us, dispel our inner darkness, and fill us with the resplendent light of His grace. *Āmīn*. May He bless us with the fullness of His qualities and actions which have neither comparison nor equal. *Amīn*.

My very precious children, let us speak further about the language and qualities of the child. My precious children, when a baby emerges from its mother, it cries, "Amma, Amma!" That sound gladdens the mother's heart and brings joy to all those nearby. Isn't it a sound which makes everyone want to pick up the child and kiss it? Isn't it a sound which makes everyone happy? Does it make people cry? Certainly not. In fact, the same kind of sound is also made by sheep, by cows, and by many other animals. No matter what language you speak, that sound brings coolness, comfort, and gladness to the heart. Even though a mother may suffer and scream in pain and torment, even though she may come close to death when giving birth, as soon as she hears the sound of the baby's cry, she is soothed, she forgets all her pain, and her heart is comforted. She lifts the child to her heart, embraces it, and kisses it as soon as she hears that sound.

In just the same way God is both our Father and our Mother. How much pain He suffers to deliver us from this world of ignorance, from this world of sin, this world of karma, this world of anger! He has such a heavy burden to endure. Indeed, He carries all our burdens for us, and He shares all our suffering and torment in this world. He shares our pain and suffers the burden of carrying us. When we emerge from this world of the five elements, this world of desire, mind, karma, anger, jealousy, and arrogance which all try to swallow us, if we say, "Amma," or, "My Father, my God!" that sound immediately soothes Him. It brings coolness and comfort, not only to God, our Father, but to all living creatures. They want to gather us to their hearts, to kiss and embrace us. Even if we have committed so many faults, so many sins, and caused so much suffering, even if we live forgetting our Father who is God, even if we despise God, even if we deny the existence of God, even if we scold God, see how tolerant He is. He continues to do His duty no matter what we do. Even though our parents may forget us, God comes to help and protect us no matter where we are. We must understand how God protects us. If we understand that, we will know how He lives with us, always helping and protecting us. We will realize ourselves and Him.

My very precious children, a newborn child speaks so many languages, but it is not understood by its mother or father or even by those who are profoundly learned. The little ones speak millions of languages—the language of the crane, the dog, the cat, the monkey, the languages of man—yet the only ones who can understand are other babies. In the first year and a half of life, an infant runs the gamut of all languages and sounds. The monkey is inside, man is inside, the entire world is there inside the baby. It speaks the language of jinns, fairies, angels, *gnānis*, and the language of God. It speaks every language, even the rustling of the ant, the buzzing of the mosquito, and the humming of the bees. The baby speaks all their languages and is a friend to every creature—the birds are its friends and it plays happily with them, even the snake is its friend. This universal language makes the baby everyone's friend. It has no prejudice and it makes no distinctions of color or whatever.

No matter where we take a baby, it knows the language of God. Others may not comprehend, but God understands. God hears the baby's voice, and every voice that floats on the wind is understood by the baby. Unity understands, compassion understands, the child understands, and all other beings understand these languages. Man alone does not understand. Why is that? Because man has changed. Man has forgotten the language that others have not.

If two babies are brought together, they speak to each other; they make some kind of noise. They understand each other and become friends. No matter what part of the world they may come from, the two of them will start to play together. They become friends no matter what color they may be. Bring a baby from the east and leave it with a baby from the west, and they will talk in their common language; bring another baby from the north or the south, and they will speak their common language. The baby understands every possible language because it understands unity, peace, happiness, and joy. That language is understood by the baby alone. It does not speak the temporary languages of the world which human beings have learned; instead it knows all the original languages and speaks with joy and happiness, without sorrow or suffering. All its languages bring unity and happiness, and the baby lives in and enjoys that unity.

Because the baby knows the language of every living creature, it can speak to any life that comes near it. The baby even has a language to converse with God. Even if we have learned all the languages of the world, if we want to converse with God we must become a baby and learn that original language, the original words, the original unity, peace, and equality, the language we spoke when we were born, the language which the world cannot recognize. We can speak to God with this language, but our mothers and fathers will not understand it; religions, racial prejudice, philosophies, scriptures, and literature will not comprehend. That language will not be understood by any knowledge that has been nurtured in the world. The world will look upon us as dreaming, blind men who cannot describe what they see. The language we spoke when we were babies is understood only by our Father who is God and by those who live in peace and equality.

When we speak this language, when we discover that equality, that peace, that justice, that unity, and that exalted state, when we are like babies, when we live as little children and behave as little children, what do we find? We find peace and tranquillity. We find the unity and love which embraces everyone. We may totter and fall while embracing each other, but we will do so in unity and love. This is the quality of our play as God's children—we play with Him, and He understands our language, our speech, and our wisdom. This is the language we can use to converse with God, our Father. These are the qualities we must have to live in His kingdom. This is His speech, these are His qualities, and this is the state in which He lives. We must acquire that state in this world. We must embrace all lives as our own life and look after every living creature as we look after ourselves, as does the baby who hands some of its food to another child or even takes food from its own mouth to give it to another. Just as babies live with these qualities in that state, we too can live with our Father if we have these qualities. This is the language He understands, this is the love He understands, this is the justice and the judgment He knows. If we have these qualities, we will understand the language we need to converse with Him.

My very precious children, that is what we call being a baby, being a little child. My very precious children, we must learn this language and acquire the good qualities and the happiness of this language. We must understand the clarity, the meaning, and the peace of this language. My precious children, the state we call infancy is a state in which we try to reach God's state, try to learn everything from God, to acquire the qualities of God, to be one with God, and to know ourselves.

We must keep on being students, learning. As long as we remain students, we are prepared to learn. As long as we live in peace, happiness, and unity, as long as we live as one race, as long as we live in harmony and unity, we can call ourselves little babies. The feeling of 'I' will have left us, ego will have left, selfishness will have left, and any sense of difference or prejudice will have left. Vanity will be gone, anger will be gone, hatred will be gone, hastiness will be gone, and the sense of my race, your race, my religion, your religion will be gone. The feeling that my language and my writing are different from yours will be gone. Just as that little baby speaks all languages in unity, we must become students and try to understand the meaning of all the languages we spoke earlier. We must understand the truth and unity in that language, the equality and happiness we perceived in it. We must extract the meaning and explanation of everything we said during that time.

My precious children, if we do become students, discarding our selfishness, our pride and vanity, our anger, the discrimination among languages and all the temporary things we learned, then we can really begin to learn. As long as we remain students, we will never grow old. As long as we are prepared to learn we will stay young, never aging. But the moment we say, "I have studied and I know," we begin to grow old. As soon as we stop being a student, we begin to age. The moment we let ourselves be praised as an important person, we grow old. When we are vain and proud, we do not allow further learning. The moment we become a teacher instead of a student, we grow old. The moment we become a swami, our learning is finished. We grow old, the Angel of Death appears, and we have to face Judgment Day. The moment we stop being a student, we age, time passes, our intelligence disappears, all the benefits of our life retreat, and we are left to face our Judgment Day.

My dear children, if we can remain as students, we will remain eternally young in the state of a baby. We will speak like a baby and grow in the protection of God, our Father. God will lift us up, embrace us, and speak to us. He understands that language, He understands that love, and He will feed us with the milk of His love. As long as we continue to learn we can dwell in the presence of God and be with Him. We will live in His presence, and it will become His duty to raise us. But the moment we become a teacher, praiseworthy, learned, a guru, a swami, we forfeit God's protection. Then what? The only thing left for us is the Angel of Death and satan instead of God. There is only hell for us after that, only maya, vanity, pride, anger, selfishness, all the praise and doubt of the world, all the treachery, deceit, trickery, and hypocrisy of saying things we do not feel. We are left with these qualities the moment we stop learning. This is hell.

If we stop learning, all the passion, anger, miserliness, envy, greed, fanaticism, arrogance, karma, maya, intoxicants, lust, murder, theft, and falsehood which left while we were learning will return to attach themselves to us again. Hell will come back to us and we will age. The Angel of Death is certain to follow, and our lives will be poured like oil onto the fires of hell. However, my precious children, as long as we are babies, as long as we are prepared to learn, we speak every language, we comprehend every language, and we are able to comfort every life. We are able to converse with every life, with the sparrows and all the birds, with cattle and goats, with snakes and scorpions. We can speak to all God's creations. As soon as they see these good qualities, God's love and His actions, as soon as they see that happiness, every creature will bow in obeisance. Birds and animals will bow down, and they will love us and come to play without fear.

We must realize that it is in this state that we can live with God and that it is truth which understands the baby's language. Only if we are like babies do we remain young. Only then do we have a place in the kingdom of God, remaining eternally young, without death, without rebirth, without perishing or being destroyed. In that state, we are not governed by time and we are without want. We are that mystery, that secret which is the only secret, the only mystery, the only power which is God, our Father. We must realize this and think about it. No matter how much we study, we must resolve to continue learning. We must want to live with our Father and be one with our Father. We must love all lives as our own, love our neighbors and our brothers as ourselves, and comfort and show compassion to every living creature. When such qualities come into us, God will understand our language. He will hear our sounds, and He will understand our speech, our wisdom, our love, our unity, and our peacefulness.

My very precious children, youth is being a student. Youth is learning. It is a state of peace and equality, a state in which we can be one with our Father and live with our Father. Youth is a state in which God who is both our Father and our Mother never leaves us. He protects us and looks after us. If we could only think about this, my very precious children, and try to live in this state, understanding what this language means. We must try to understand and speak that language. Then God will understand. That is the baby's state, the student's state. We must be

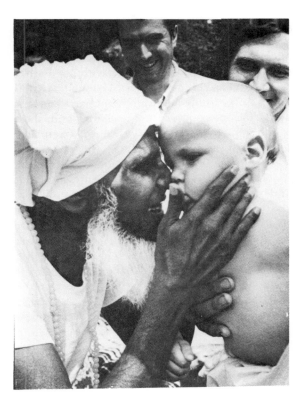

eternal babies and learn the language of heaven, the secrets of heaven, the secrets of God, God's qualities, His actions, and the wealth of His grace. We must learn the mystery that is God's. We must learn every aspect of His qualities and duties, everything about Him, everything He does. God speaks every language and feeds each of His creations according to its need. He speaks to each life and each creation. We, too, must learn to speak that language again.

But when we do this the world will not understand. People with racial or color prejudice and people with religious bias will not understand. This language is not understood by the world or by worldly institutions. They will say, "We don't know what this baby is babbling about. He is talking unintelligibly. But never mind, let's show our love to him, pat him on the head, and move on." We can be certain that the language we use to talk to God will not be understood by the world. Our present state of ignorance, passion, and arrogance will not understand that language. Our envy, our racial and color prejudice, our fanaticism, our bigotry, and the knowledge we have acquired from books will not understand. Only when we become babies and continue to learn will we understand. This is the way to acquire eternal youth. If we remain as babies and keep learning, we will live in the presence of God, our Father. If we try to become wise, we will live with our Father and we will never leave Him, we will never need to say farewell. Then we will be able to speak to our Father, we will understand His language, and He will give us His commandments.

However, my dearest children, if we say, "I am great," or "These are mine," if we proudly say, "I have studied, I am a leader, I have status and influence, I have come to rule the world," then by praising ourselves we separate ourselves from God; we leave our Father and go to hell. As long as we stay with Him, we are a baby and a student, we have patience, equality, peacefulness, and tolerance. But if we leave that state, we pass into divisiveness, doubt, suspicions, the desire of satan, and the antics and pranks of the monkey-mind. We are fascinated by the hypnotic display of maya. It is a time of darkness when we desire earth, gold, and sensual pleasures, and we are divided from God, our Father. We must work hard to stay with Him, to be little children willing to learn, willing to ask our Father, willing to learn His language.

My very precious children, jeweled lights of my eyes who are the life within my life, we must think about this. We are wasting our lives. Shouldn't we always be like little babies? Shouldn't we always stay with our Father? Shouldn't we remain with our Father, never leaving Him? The only time we have any happiness is when we are with Him. When we have understanding, we have unity and peace. Whether there is joy or sorrow, we live happily and harmoniously with everyone, speaking and understanding every language, realizing everything. That time of babyhood is eternal youth, when we have that beauty of the heart and body, that beauty of the face, the beauty of wisdom, and the beauty of unity, and everyone picks us up to embrace us with love.

We must not forfeit our youth and be transformed into an old age of vanity, pride, and qualities which are not God's. That is what old age is: the qualities of satan, a dark, black face, a face which speaks with envy and jealousy and reveals the qualities of the dog of desire and the monkey which makes us say what we do not feel inside. It is a hard, black, granite heart without compassion, riddled with holes where snakes live. God does not dwell in a place where there is so much darkness. God's qualities are like the baby's, but satan's qualities are those of pride. God's qualities, His language, and His speech bring comfort and peace. They display compassion for everyone. His language is the language of love, of grace and unity, the language which speaks to all creations, which plays with everyone and makes them happy. This is God's love. Satan's love is discrimination, differences, murder, separations, I am greater than you, I am bigger than you, desire for praise, treachery, vengeance, the qualities of the lion, the tiger, and the bear, killing one another, eating another life. These divisive forces which attack and hurt others, these qualities of hell which tear others to bits and eat them, these qualities of fire which burn everything—these are the qualities of satan, the qualities which point to the aging which points to death and burning in hell. These are the qualities which divide us from God.

My very dear children, let us think about this separation from our Father. The secret of not separating from our Father is to remain a student, a baby who knows all languages. Those who are older are separated from that speech, from those good qualities, and from their Father. They have gone to hell. We must realize that there are endless secrets to be learned about our Father, about His limitless love, and about the infinite, undiminishing wealth of His grace. His mystery is far beyond our wisdom. There is so much to learn, so much to investigate within His mystery, His wealth, His grace, His infinite duties, and the joy of those duties. There is so much to see and learn. To learn all this we must be students, we must go on learning, we must remain as babies. As we become young and stay young, we acquire that beauty, and as we go on learning, the love of our Father grows inside us. As that love grows, He embraces us more and more. As He holds us closer, more of His light pours into us, and as that light pours into us, the darkness recedes and we receive the love of every creation. We must think about this.

Precious children, jeweled lights of my eyes, always keep trying to regain that eternal youth so that you can learn from God, our Father. He knows and understands your language. Learn that language which is your Father's; then you will understand Him. Let us remain eternally young through that common language and never leave our Father. The world will not understand, even our own father and mother will not understand. No one except God will comprehend that language, that secret, the secret of your prayers, the secret of your learning, the secret of the wealth of His grace, of unity, of peace, of equality, the secret of your life, the secret of your Father, the secret of never perishing, of never dying, of having no birth, no death, the secret of eternal youth. These are the secrets you will learn if you are eternally a student. These are secrets no one else knows.

My very dear children, if you want to attain

that state of peace and tranquillity, you must learn the language of God, your Father. He alone will understand; others will not. Let the world keep its books, its languages and separations. God does not understand the languages the world uses. The language spoken by one person is not understood by the next; this is the way of the world. Only satan can make sense of these divisive languages, but what a true student says is understood by God. Every child must think about this. My very precious children, jeweled lights of my eyes, if we do this as babies, if we reflect on this as babies, we will achieve the benefit of this birth, eternal youth, peace, and equality. Every child, please think about this.

Just as electricity is extracted from water, just as we breathe in a tiny magnetic bit from the air which sustains life, just as we discover precious gems buried in the earth, just as we take the light from the sun and draw the coolness of the moon through the ether, we must throw away the darkness of our desires and extract that tiny atom of God's grace and wealth. Just as we extract the essence of the five elements, earth, fire, water, air, and ether, we must extract peace from the body, compassion from God, and learning from His mystery. This is the way to understand with wisdom, the way to develop the wisdom which extracts the essence of each thing. We must use the wisdom we have to understand each thing, extract its essence, and learn from it. We must learn, my very precious children. We must take the necessary understanding from every book we read. We must take the point from every letter we look at. We must extract the essence of everything we see just as we extract and use the essence of the medicine we might take. Even if we are ill, we must discard the pain and take in only peace and understanding. In just this way, my very precious children, a little baby takes in only the point. Like that, we must take in that point of God's qualities from everything we see, extracting only the point and discarding everything else.

Just as we are unable to understand what a baby says, the world does not understand what God says. Only those who are the right age can do that. When a baby speaks God hears, and when God speaks the baby understands. We must develop that embracing love, that peacefulness which has no selfishness. But only that point will understand, my dearest children, and that is called youth, eternal youth. Only then are we young. Only then are we students living with our Father as young children must.

We must remember, my precious children, if we stay in the presence of our Father our beauty will never fade, we will never age. Our sense of unity, of peacefulness, justice, duty, and righteousness will never leave us. As long as we have that beauty, we will never age and our bodies will never change or grow old. Please think about this, my very dear children. This is what we have to learn. This is what we have to extract and understand from all that we do. To understand this and to be students, we must begin to understand the language of God. We spoke it when we were infants, didn't we? That is the language that cools every heart. The words we used in the first year or two of life were God's language and God's qualities. We must transform ourselves into students of that age; only then will we understand the mysterious secret of God's wisdom, His qualities, and His actions.

My dearest children, be quite certain that as long as we fail to reach that state of babyhood we are divided from God and we are aging. We must not accept this aging that separates us from God. We must not take on those qualities that keep us from Him. Instead we should try to hold on to the youthfulness which keeps us with God and never separates us from Him. Then we will remain in our Father's kingdom. The moment we leave Him, we are in the kingdom of hell. We should never leave His presence or His kingdom.

Precious children, each one of you please think about this and try to establish this state. Please be students living with our Father, taking on His qualities. Try to acquire wisdom in a state of freedom and liberation. This is the state of our soul, the freedom of our soul, the resplendent light of freedom. We must not waste our time or throw it away. We must use it to learn the speech and the qualities of our Father. Let us try very hard to remain with Him and never leave.

May we live as students always in His presence. May every child reflect on this. My precious children, try to learn that language, and never, never think of yourself as great or famous. As long as there is more to investigate, we are students. The moment we complete all our research we become God and we receive the kingdom of God. But until our research is finished we must continue to learn, and the only way to truly learn is to remain with Him. He is the king, and you must remain with Him as His young prince or princess, learning as a student until He crowns you. We must learn. We must try to attain this peace and equality with God's qualities and unity. That is the best kind of learning.

The language our Father understands, the language the baby understands, is understood by no one else. Truth is not understood by the world, by books, by religions or philosophies. The speech of the eternal student, the eternal youth, is no more intelligible to the world than a baby's. That one mysterious language is the mystery we must try to learn. My precious children, as you continue to understand more and more, the world might bite you, scold you, or chase you away. Even a mother doesn't understand the baby's language, but that is the way of the world. Until the baby learns what the mother imposes on it and says what the mother wants, until the mother makes the baby think as she thinks and speak her own language, she does not understand. Until then only God, the true Father, understands.

God provides the language, the understanding, the food, the truth, the freedom, the liberation of the soul, justice, and judgment. This is what we must learn from our Father. No one else will understand; the world will never understand that language. Why not? Because the world only knows the temporary languages it learns for this temporary life. The world will only understand if we speak its language. If we remain with God, only He will understand.

My very precious children, may we understand this and find a way to search for wisdom, to have peace of mind, lasting happiness, and the kingdom of heaven. May we find a way to stay there eternally. *Āmīn*. May God grant us this blessing with His grace. All wealth, all grace is with God, our Father. All wisdom, all treasures are His. The age of eternal youth is with Him. May we reach that age of no separation from Him, may we take on the beauty of being students, may we understand that subtle mystery. *Āmīn*.

May God bless us with His grace and His qualities. *Āmīn*. May He bless us with His actions. *Āmīn*. May He bless us with His conduct and His unity, may He give us His compassion, and may He give us truth and that life which never leaves Him. May He gather us to His heart, accept us as babies, and protect us. *Āmīn*.

Glossary

(A) indicates an Arabic word. (T) indicates Tamil.

al-hamdu lillāh (A) All praises to You. The glory
and greatness that deserves praise is Allah. You
are the One responsible for the appearance of
all creations. Whatever appears, whatever perishes, whatever receives benefit or loss—all is
Yours. I have surrendered everything into Your
hands. I remain with hands outstretched,
empty, and helpless. Whatever is happening
and whatever is going to happen is all Yours.
Lit.: All praise is to and of Allah!

Āmīn (A) So be it. May He make this complete.

amma (T) Mother

*As-Salāmu 'alaikum wa rahmatullāhi wa barakātuhu
kuiluhu* (A) May the peace of God and His beneficence be upon all of you!

Bismillāhir-Rahmānir-Rahīm (A) *Bismillāh*: Allah
is the first and the last. The One with the beginning, and the One without beginning. He is the
One who is the cause for creation and for the
absence of creation, the cause for the beginning

and for the beginningless. *Ar-Rahmān*: He is the King. He is the Nourisher, the One who gives food. He is the Compassionate One. He is the One who protects the creations. He is the Beneficent One. *Ar-Rahīm*: He is the One who redeems; the One who protects from evil, who preserves and who confers eternal bliss; the Savior. On the day of judgment and on the day of inquiry and on all days from the day of the beginning, He protects and brings His creations back to Himself. Lit.: In the name of God, Most Merciful, Most Compassionate.

gnāni (T) A man of wisdom; one who has *gnānam*; one who has received the qualities and wisdom of God by surrendering to God and who lives in a state of peace and equality where he sees all lives as equal; one who has attained the state of peace.

'ibādat (A) Prayer; worship and service to the One God.

In the many languages there are many common words such as prayer, *pūjās*, meditation, and worship. In Arabic the term is *'ibādat*. But true *'ibādat* is when the heart melts like molten wax and is in prayer to the One God. Only that state can truly be called prayer.

110

ill-Allāhu (A)   See: *Lā ilāha ill-Allāhu*

īmān (A)   Absolute, complete and unshakable faith, certitude, and determination that God alone exists; the complete acceptance of the heart that God is One.

karma (T)   The inherited qualities formed at the time of conception; the qualities of the essences of the five elements; the qualities of the mind; the qualities of the connection to hell.

The qualities and actions of the seventeen *purānas*—arrogance, karma, maya [illusion]; *tārahan*, *singhan*, and *sūran*, the three sons of maya representing the sexual energies; the six intrinsic evils of lust, anger, miserliness, attachment, fanaticism, and envy; and the five acquired evils of intoxication, obsession, theft, murder, and falsehood.

La ilāha ill-Allāhu (A)   There are two aspects: *La ilāha* is the manifestation of creation [*sifāt*]. *Ill-Allāhu* is the essence [*dhāt*]. All that has appeared, all creation, belongs to *Lā ilāha*. The One who created all that, His name is *Allāhu*. "Other than You there is no God. Only You are Allah." To accept this with certitude, to strengthen one's *īmān*, and to affirm this

111

Kalimah—this is the state of Islam. Lit.: There is nothing other than You, Only You are God.

māya (T) Illusion; the unreality of the visible world; the glitters seen in the darkness of illusion; the 105 million glitters seen in the darkness of the mind which result in 105 million rebirths.

   Maya is an energy or sakti which takes on various shapes, makes man forfeit his wisdom, and confuses and hypnotizes him into a state of torpor. It can take many, many millions of hypnotic forms. If man tries to grasp one of these forms with his intellect, he will see it but he will never be able to catch it, for it will take on yet another form.

qalb (A) The heart within the heart of man; the inner heart. His Holiness explains that there are two states for the *qalb* and four chambers. The four chambers are earth, fire, air, and water, representing Hinduism, Fire Worship, Christianity, and Islam. Inside these four chambers there is a flower, the flower of the *qalb*, which is the divine qualities of God. It is the flower of grace. His fragrance exists only in this *qalb*. The four chambers are black; they are really the dog [*kalb*], the black dog which is the world, the thought of the world and the five elements.

But Allah's truth and His fragrance is that flower of the heart. That is the kingdom of Allah's church or mosque. There are some who worship in the darkness and some who worship in the light. Those who worship within that flower worship in the light. One section is light and the other four are night.

Qutb (A)   Divine wisdom, divine analytic wisdom, the wisdom which explains; that which measures the length and breadth of the seven oceans of desires; that which awakens all the truths which have been destroyed and buried in the ocean of illusion; that which awakens true *īmān*; that which explains the state of purity to each life in the same way that it existed in the beginning of creation. The grace of the essence of God, which gives the life of purity back and which makes it into the divine vibration.

It is also a name which has been given to Allah. He can be addressed as *Yā Qutb* or *Yā Quddūs* [the Holy One]. *Quddūs* is His *wilāyat* [power or miracle], while *Qutb* is His action. *Wilāyat* is the power of that action.

Lit.: axis, axle, pole, pivot. A title used for the great holy men of Islam.

Rabb (A)   God; the Lord; the Creator and Protector.

113

rasūl (A)   Apostle or messenger. One who has wisdom, faith in God, and good qualities. One who behaves with respect and dignity toward his fellow man. A *rasūl* is one who has accepted only God and has rejected everything else, one who has accepted God's divine words, His qualities and actions and puts them into practice. Those who from time immemorial have been giving the divine laws of God to the people. Those who have such a connection with God have been called a prophet [*nabī*] or *rasūl*. The name *rasūl* has been given even to the angels.

Yā Rasūl or the Rasūlullāh is a name given to Prophet Muhammad (*Sal.*)

sabūr (A)   Inner patience; to go within patience, to practice it, to think and reflect within it.

Sabūr is that patience deep within patience which comforts, soothes, and alleviates mental suffering. The next stage is *shukūr*, or contentment. *Shukūr* is deep within *sabūr*, pacifying and comforting. Even deeper within *shukur*, still more soothing and comforting, is *tawakkal-Allāh*, absolute trust in Allah. And deep within *tawakkal-Allāh*, giving comfort and contentment, is *Al-hamdu lillāh*—surrendering all responsibility to Him. "There is nothing left in my hands." Total surrender. "I have given up everything, I am helpless, I am undone."

Sabūr, shukūr, tawakkal-Allāh, al-hamdu lillāh—these are the treasures of *īmān*. The wealth of patience is the preface to *īmān* and is the exalted wisdom in the life of a true man. To possess these four and to act by them are the four most important duties [*fards*] for *Īmān-Islām*.

Yā Sabūr—one of the 99 names of Allah. God, who is in a state of limitless patience, forgives the faults of His created beings and continues to protect them.

shukūr (A)   Contentment; the state within the inner patience known as *sabūr*; that which is kept within the treasure chest of patience. *Yā Shakūr* —one of the 99 beautiful names of Allah. To have *shukūr* with the help of the One who is *Yā Shakūr*, is true *shukūr*.

tawakkul (A)   Absolute trust and surrender; handing over to God the entire responsibility for everything. Same as *Allāhu Wakīl*—You are my Trustee, my Lawyer, my Guardian.

Index

Books by M. R. Bawa Muhaiyaddeen

Truth & Light, brief explanations
Songs of God's Grace
The Divine Luminous Wisdom That Dispels the Darkness
Wisdom of the Divine (Vols. 1-5)
The Guidebook to the True Secret of the Heart (Vols. 1, 2)
God, His Prophets and His Children
Four Steps to Pure Iman
The Wisdom of Man
A Book of God's Love
My Love You My Children:
101 Stories for Children of All Ages
Come to the Secret Garden: Sufi Tales of Wisdom
The Golden Words of a Sufi Sheikh
The Tasty, Economical Cookbook (Vols. 1, 2)
Sheikh and Disciple
Maya Veeram or The Forces of Illusion
Asma'ul-Husna: The 99 Beautiful Names of Allah
Islam and World Peace: Explanations of a Sufi
A Mystical Journey
Questions of Life-Answers of Wisdom
Treasures of the Heart: Sufi Stories for Young Children
To Die Before Death: The Sufi Way of Life
A Song of Muhammad ﷺ
Hajj: The Inner Pilgrimage

<u>For free catalog or book information call:</u>
(888) 786-1786

<u>About the Bawa Muhaiyaddeen Fellowship</u>

Muhammad Raheem Bawa Muhaiyaddeen, a Sufi mystic from Sri Lanka, was a man of extraordinary wisdom and compassion. For over seventy years he shared his knowledge and experience with people of every race and religion and from all walks of life.

The central branch of The Bawa Muhaiyaddeen Fellowship is located in Philadelphia, Pennsylvania. It was Bawa Muhaiyaddeen's residence while he was in the United States until his death in December 1986. The Fellowship continues to serve as a meeting house and a reservoir of people and materials for all who are interested in his teachings.

Also located on the same property is The Mosque of Shaikh Muhammad Raheem Bawa Muhaiyaddeen where the daily five times of prayer and Friday congregational prayers are held. An hour west of the Fellowship is the *Mazar,* or tomb, of M. R. Bawa Muhaiyaddeen which is open for visitation.

For further information write or phone:
The Bawa Muhaiyaddeen Fellowship
5820 Overbrook Avenue
Philadelphia, Pennsylvania 19131
(215)879-8604 (24 hour answering machine)
E-mai/Address: info@bmf.org   *Web Address*: http://www.bmf.org

If you would like to visit the Fellowship or obtain a schedule of current events or branch locations and meetings, please write, phone, or E-mail *Attn: Visitor Information.*